Report And Accompanying Documents Of The Virginia Commissioners Appointed To Ascertain The Bounary Line Between Maryland And Virginia

Virginia. Commission on boundary lines (1870-1874) [from old catalog]

Nabu Public Domain Reprints:

You are holding a reproduction of an original work published before 1923 that is in the public domain in the United States of America, and possibly other countries. You may freely copy and distribute this work as no entity (individual or corporate) has a copyright on the body of the work. This book may contain prior copyright references, and library stamps (as most of these works were scanned from library copies). These have been scanned and retained as part of the historical artifact.

This book may have occasional imperfections such as missing or blurred pages, poor pictures, errant marks, etc. that were either part of the original artifact, or were introduced by the scanning process. We believe this work is culturally important, and despite the imperfections, have elected to bring it back into print as part of our continuing commitment to the preservation of printed works worldwide. We appreciate your understanding of the imperfections in the preservation process, and hope you enjoy this valuable book.

TO

ACCOMPANY

THE

REPORT OF THE COMMISSIONERS

ON THE

BOUNDARY LINE

BETWEEN

VIRGINIA AND MARYLAND.

RICHMOND:
R. F. WALKER, SUPERINTENDENT PUBLIC PRINTING.
1873.

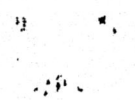

DIEV ET MON DROIT.

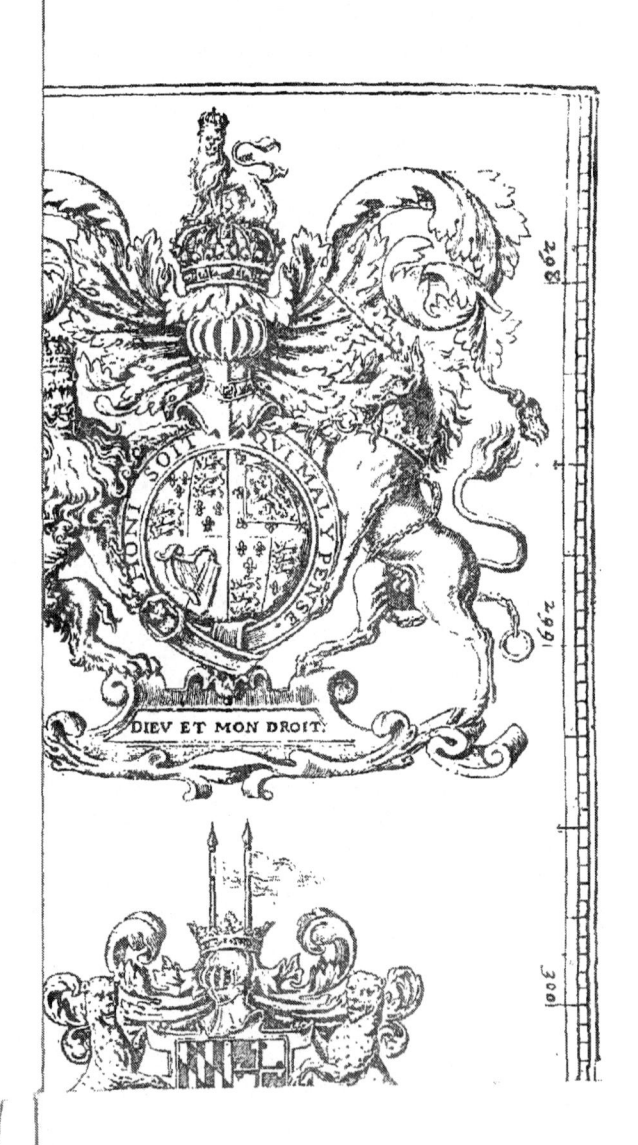

This Northerne part of Virginia (the limitts whereof extend many degrees farther Southwards) is heere inserted for the better description of the entrance into the Bay of Chesapeack
Noua TERRÆ-MARIÆ tabula
V I R G I N I Æ P A R S
CHE SA P E ACK bay
OCEANVS ORIENTALIS
DIEV ET MON DROIT
James towne
Point Comfort
Cedar poynt
S. Clement Ile
Heron Iland
Patuxent
Accomack
Sasquehannocks
Delaware Bay
W
S
E
N
A N
P

I

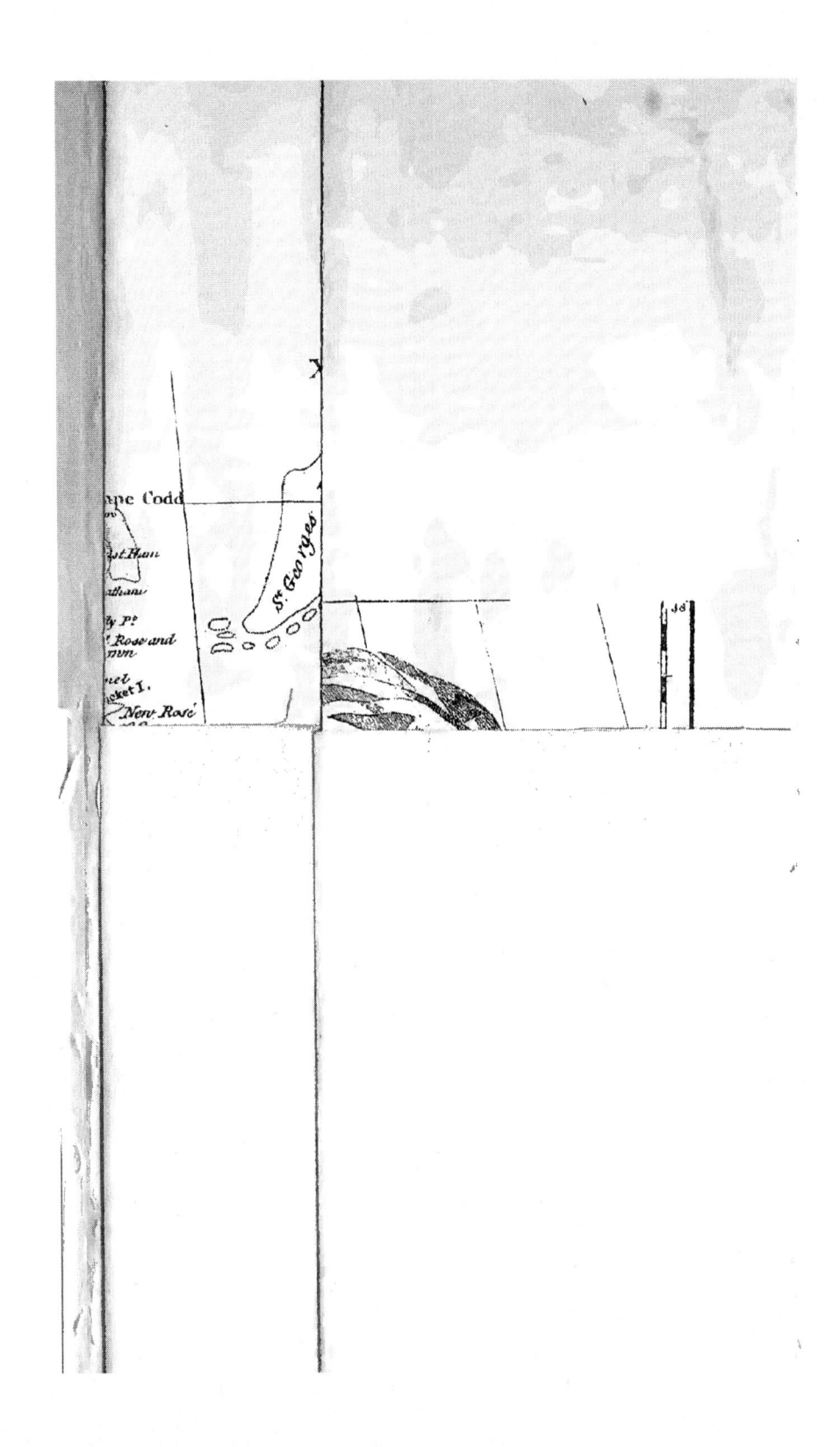

ape Codd
stHam
atham
ly P?
Rose and
wn
net
ket I.
New Rose

St Georges.

MASSACHUSETS
BAY
CONNECTICUT
Cape Cod
Nantucket Shoals
St Georges Bank
A T L
A

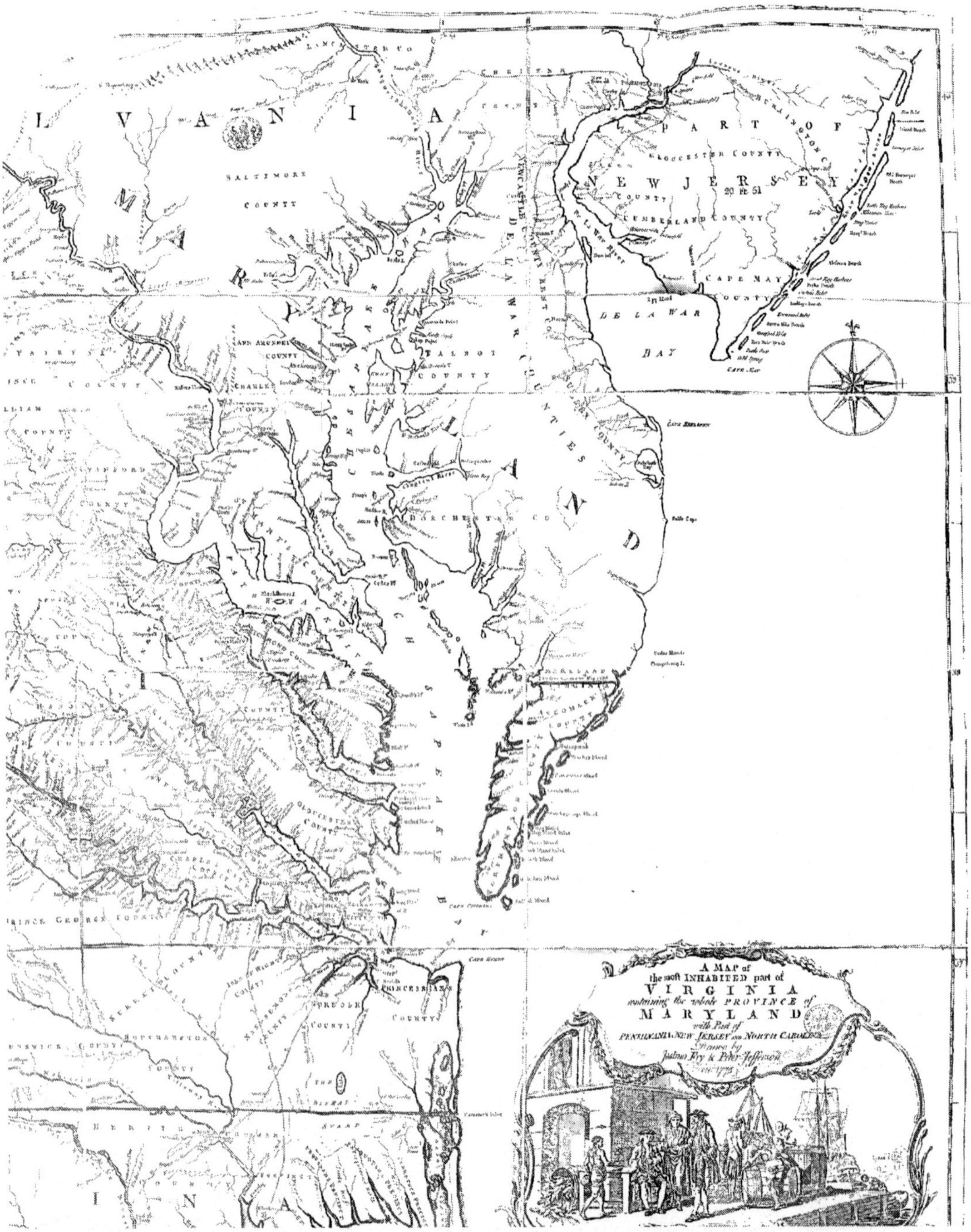

A MAP of
the most INHABITED part of
VIRGINIA
containing the whole PROVINCE of
MARYLAND
with Part of
PENSILVANIA, NEW JERSEY and NORTH CAROLINA
Drawn by
Joshua Fry & Peter Jefferson
PART OF NEW JERSEY
GLOCESTER COUNTY
CUMBERLAND COUNTY
CAPE MAY COUNTY
DE LA WAR BAY
BALTIMORE COUNTY
ANN ARUNDEL COUNTY
TALBOT COUNTY
CHARLES COUNTY
GLOUCESTER COUNTY
PRINCE GEORGE COUNTY
PRINCESS ANNE

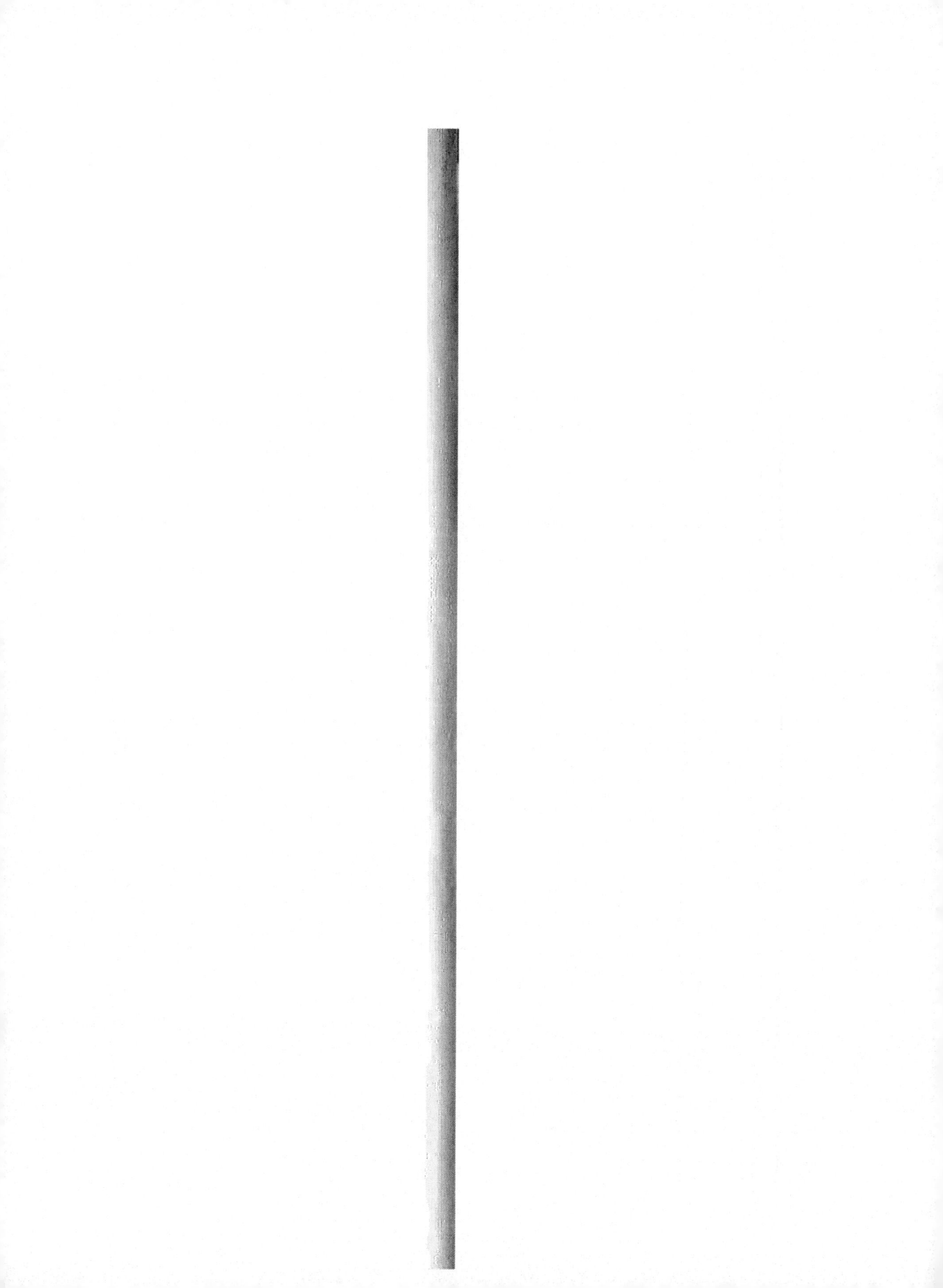

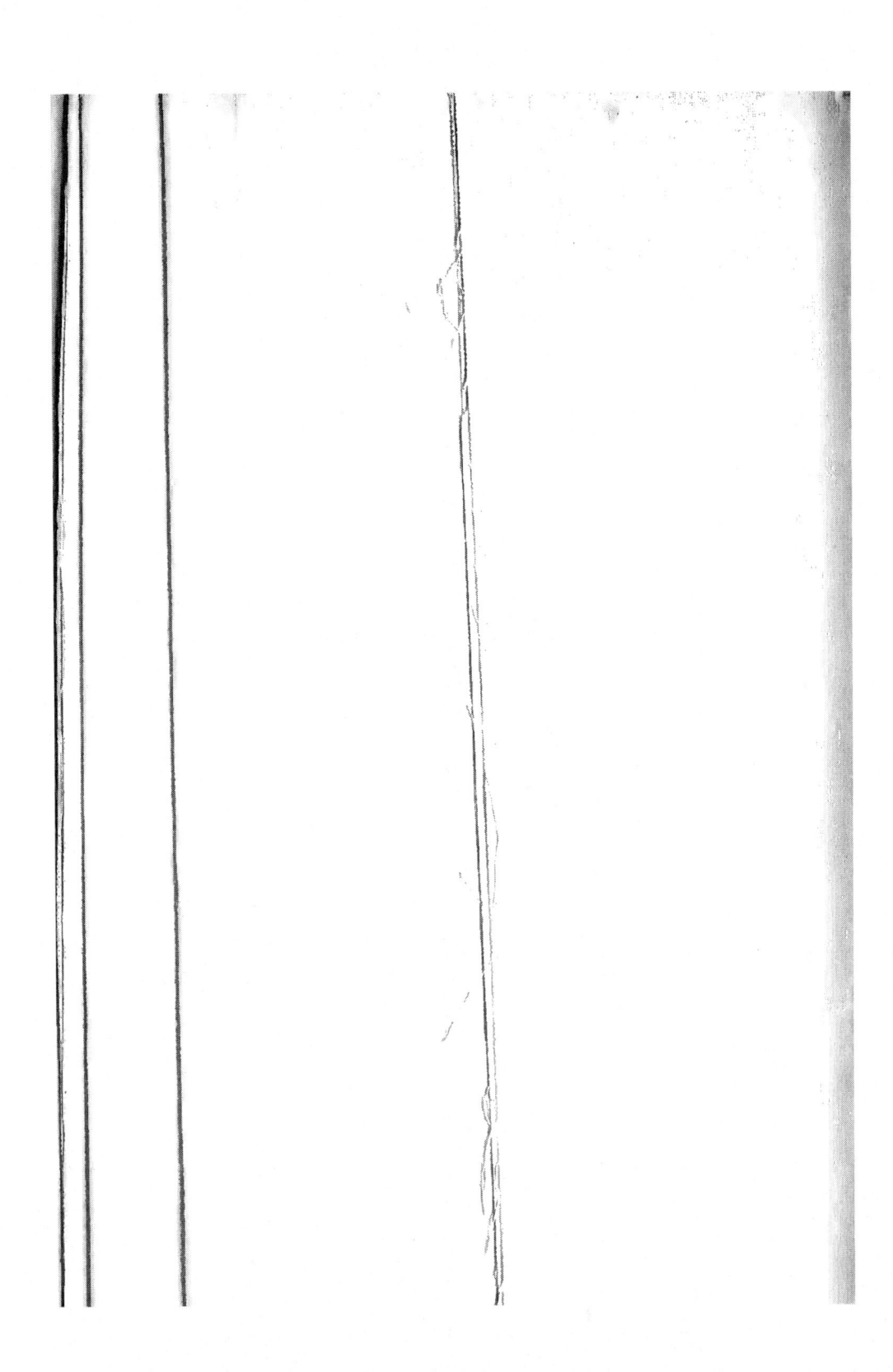

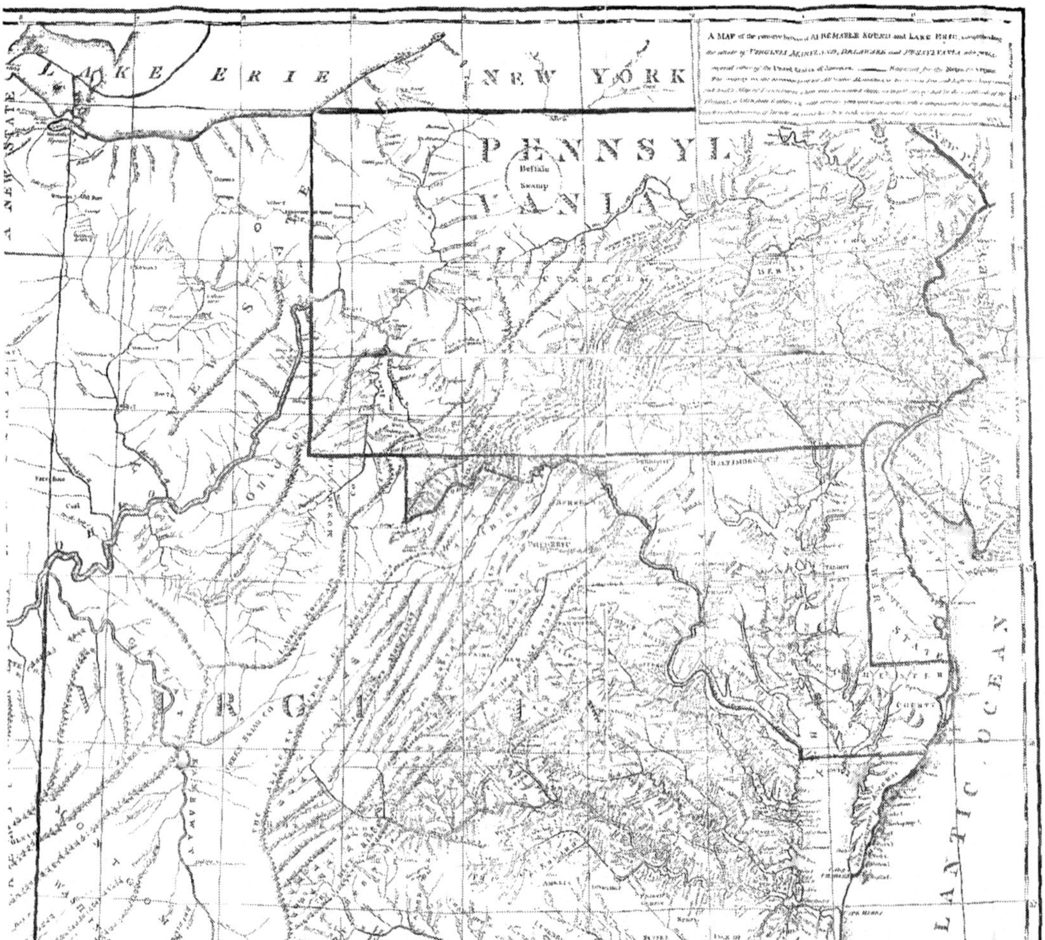

LAKE ERIE
NEW YORK
PENNSYLVANIA
Buffalo Swamp
ATLANTIC OCEAN

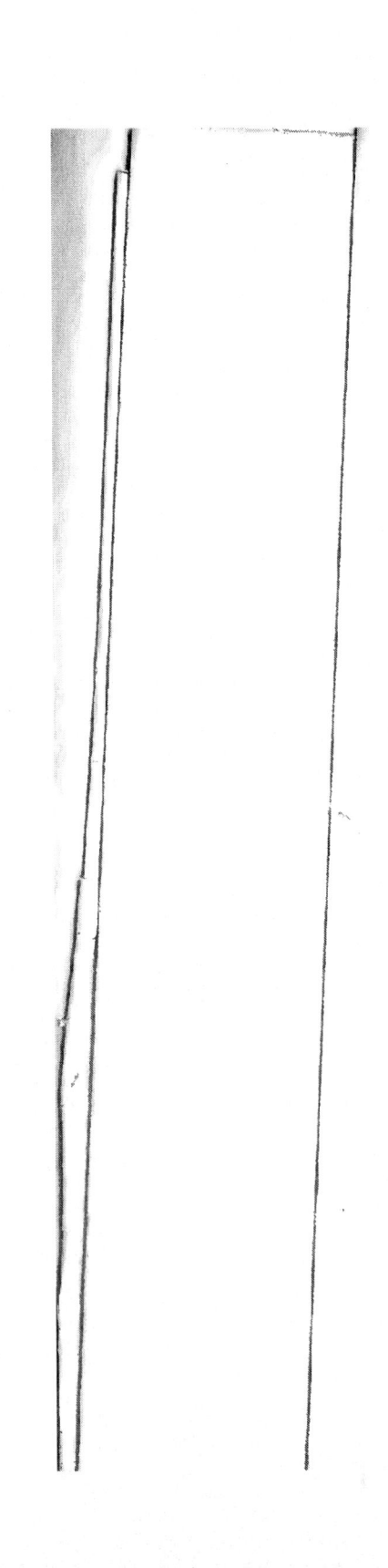

A Compleat Map of NORTH-CAROLINA *from an actual Survey*

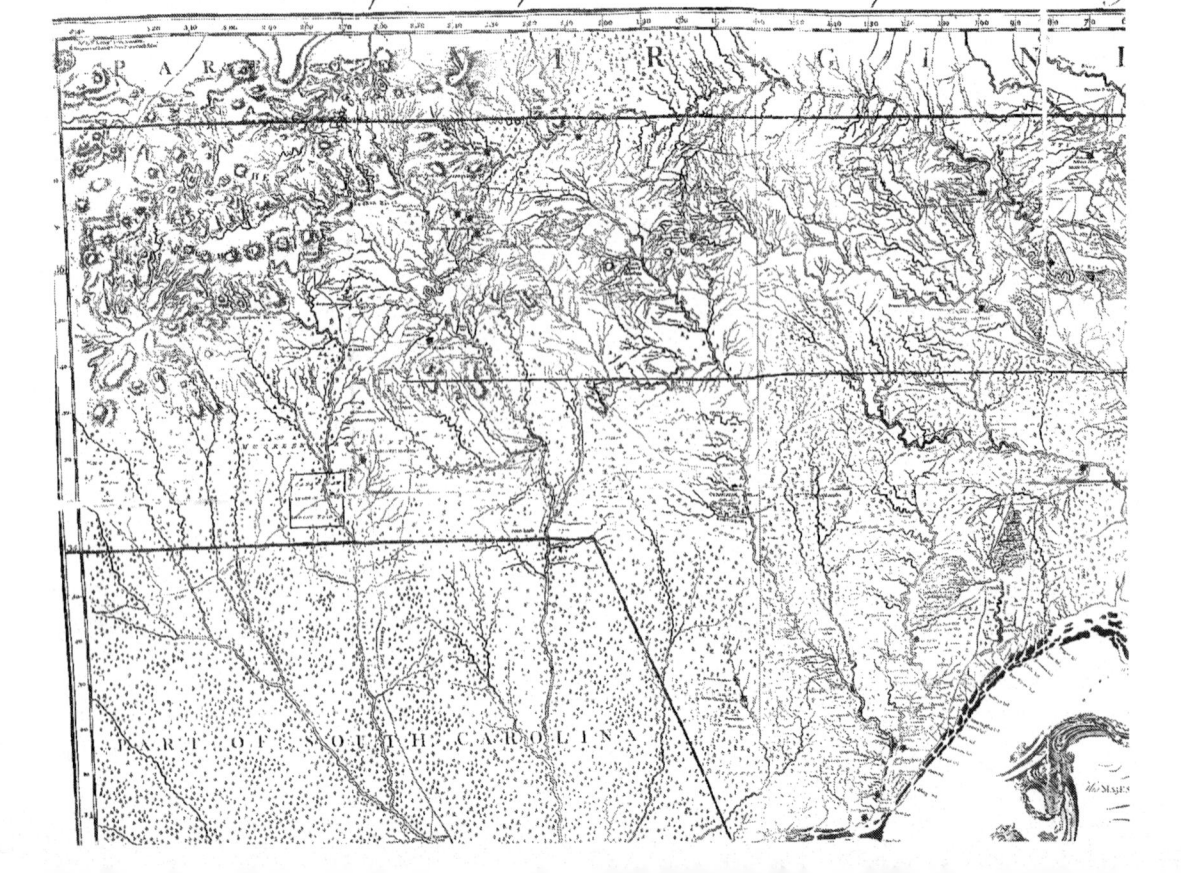

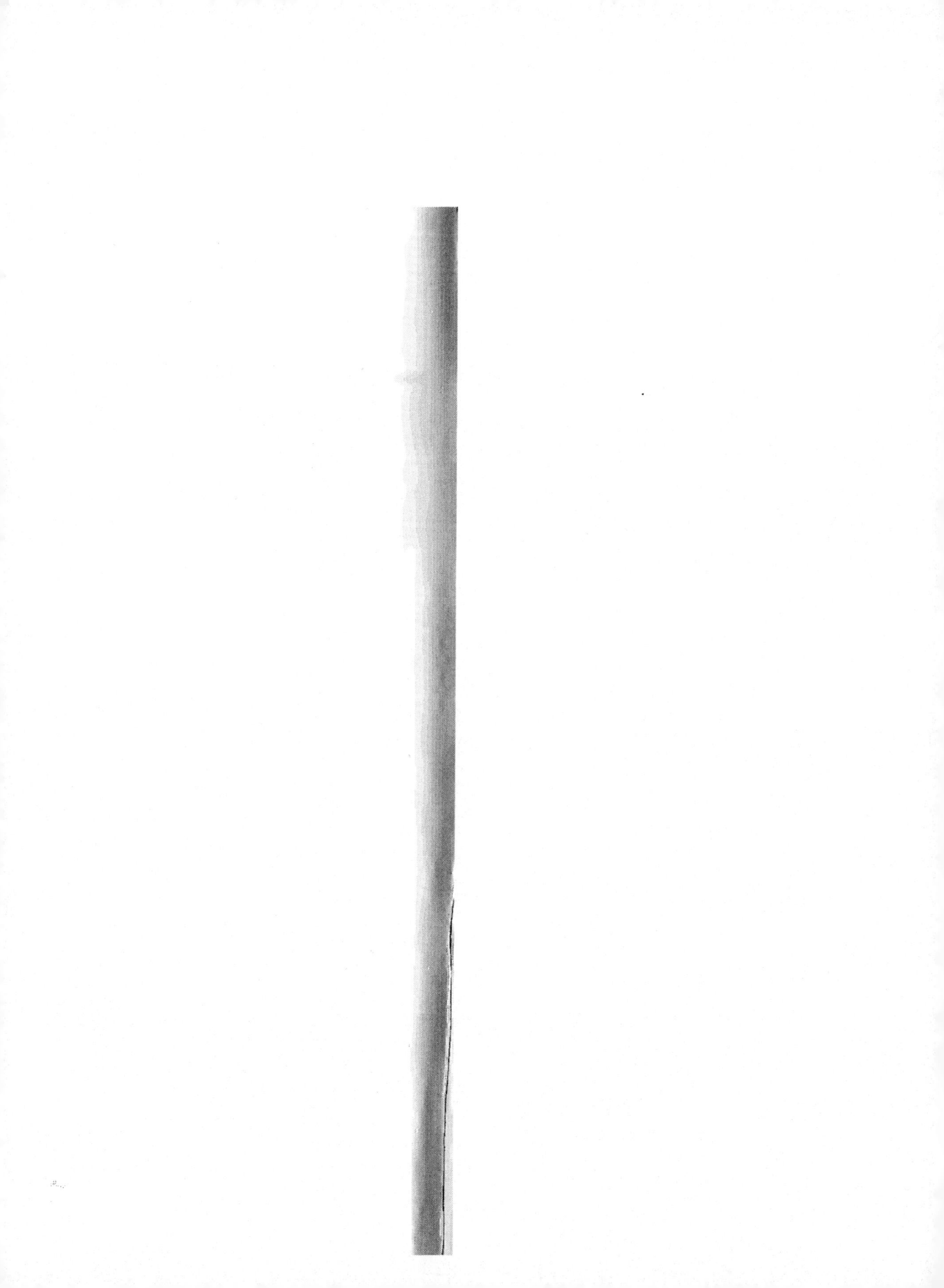

TERRA de LABRADOR
NEW BRITAIN
GULF OF ST LAURENCE
NEW FOUND LAND
THE GREAT BANK OF NEW FOUND LAND
Nova Scotia Fishing Banks
L. ONTARIO or CATARAKUI
W E S T E R N
A New and Accurate MAP OF NORTH AMERICA
Describing and distinguishing the BRITISH and SPANISH Dominions on this great Continent according to the Definitive Treaty Concluded at Paris 10th Feb. 1763.
Also all the WEST INDIA ISLANDS Belonging to, and possessed by the Several European Princes and States.
The whole laid down according to the latest and Most authentick Improvements
Eman. Bowen Geog. to His MAJESTY And John Gibson Engraver
IVth Article of the Definitive Treaty.
Vth Article of the Definitive Treaty.

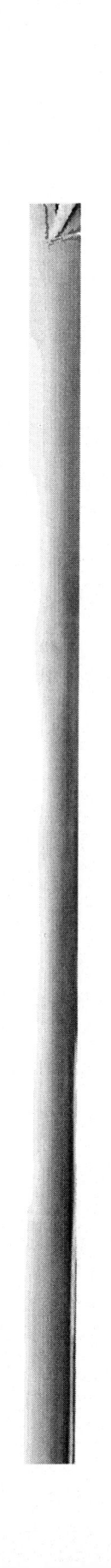

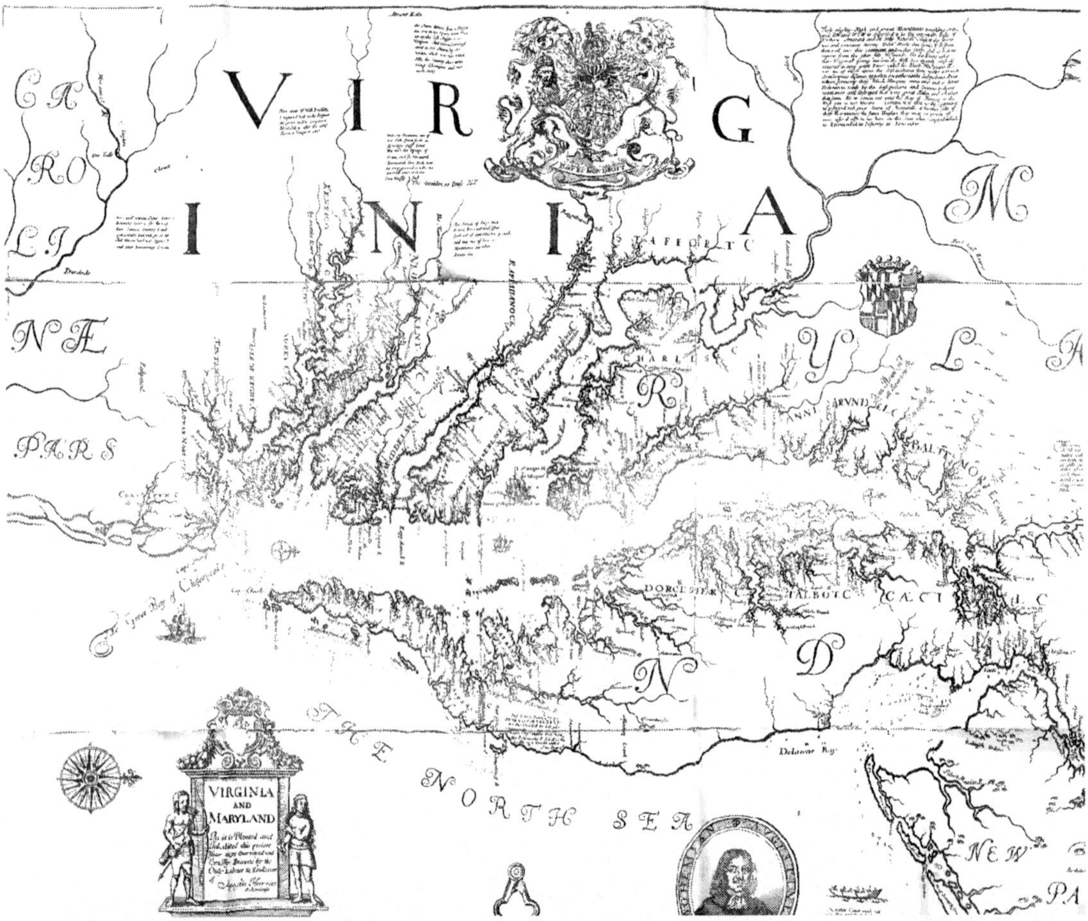
VIRGINIA
MARYLAND
CAROLINÆ PARS
CHARLES
ANNARUNDEL
BALTIMORE
DORCESTER
TALBOT
Delaware Bay
THE NORTH SEA
NEW
VIRGINIA AND MARYLAND

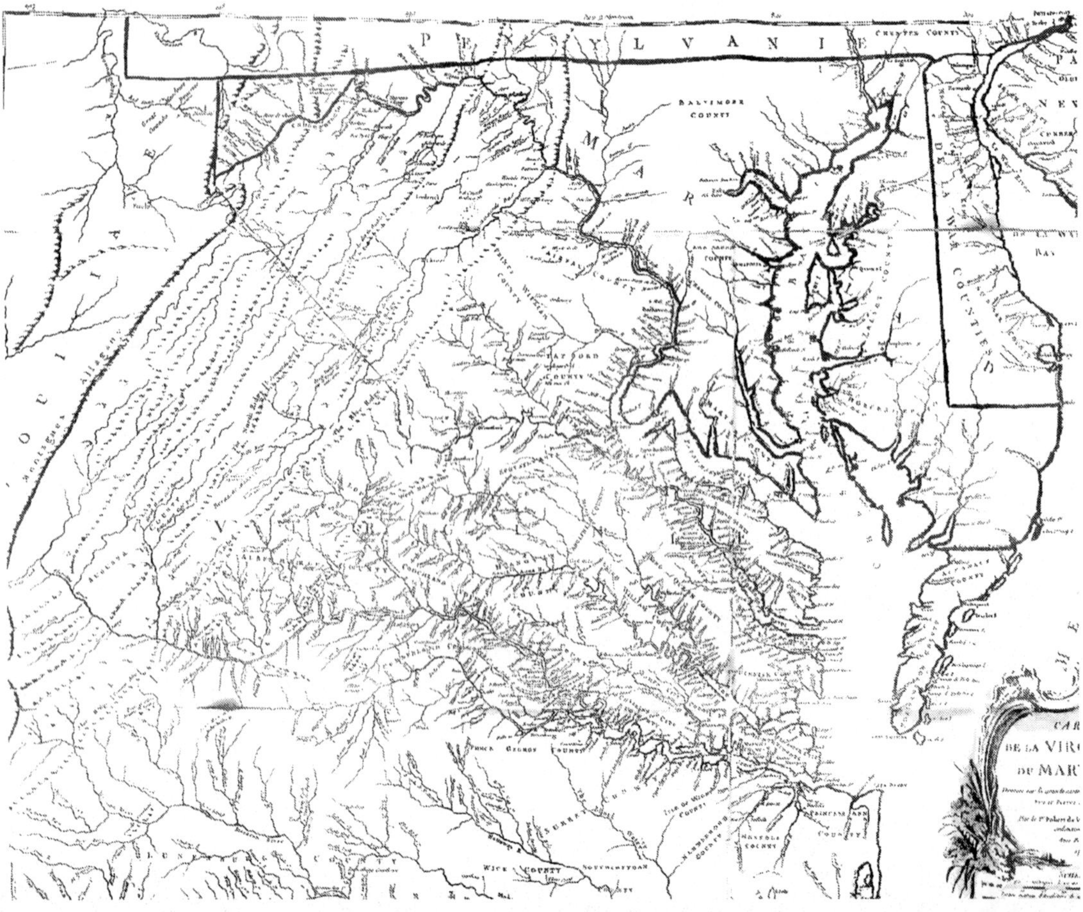
P E N S Y L V A N I E
CHESTER COUNTY
BALTIMORE COUNTY

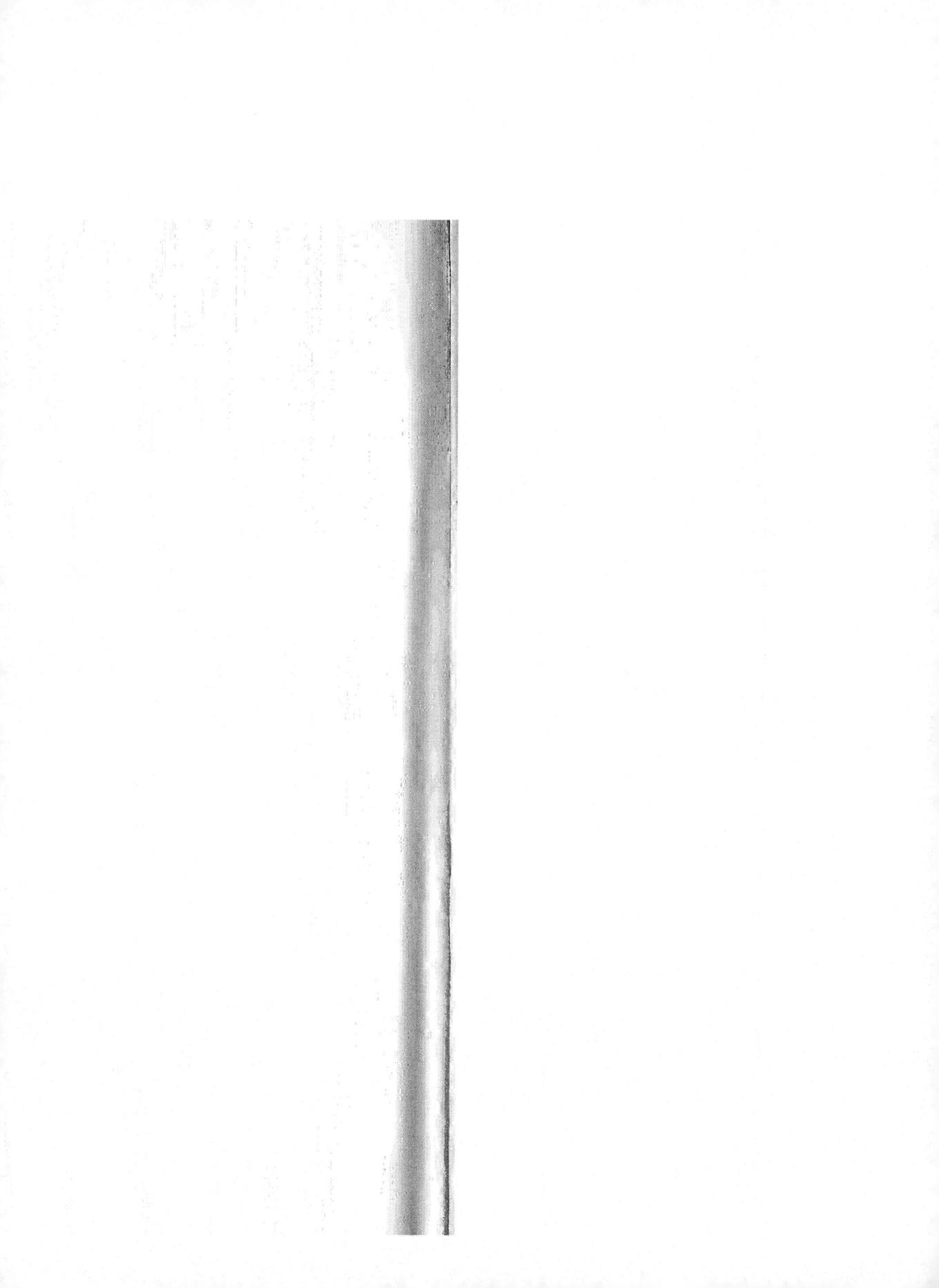

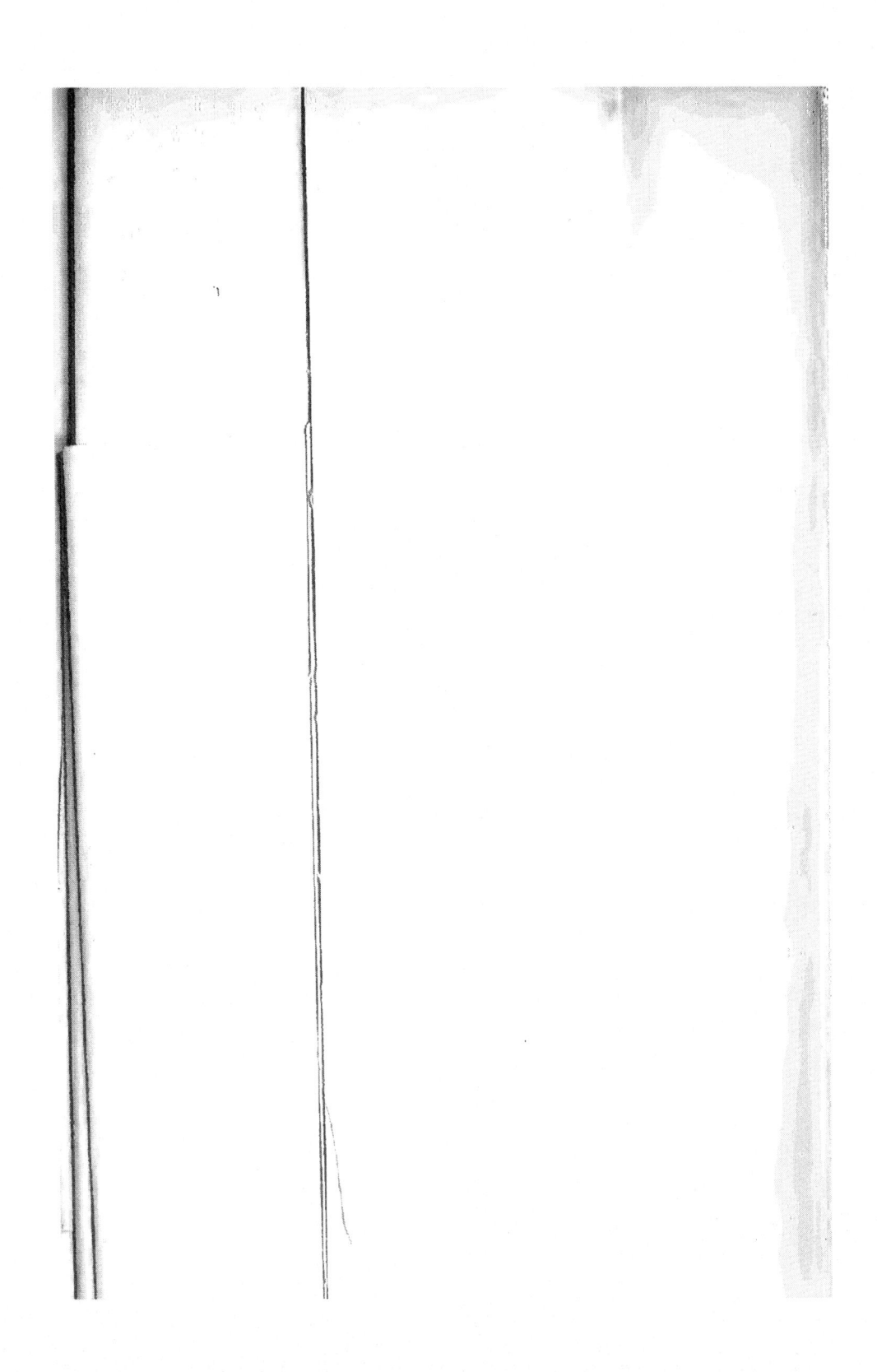

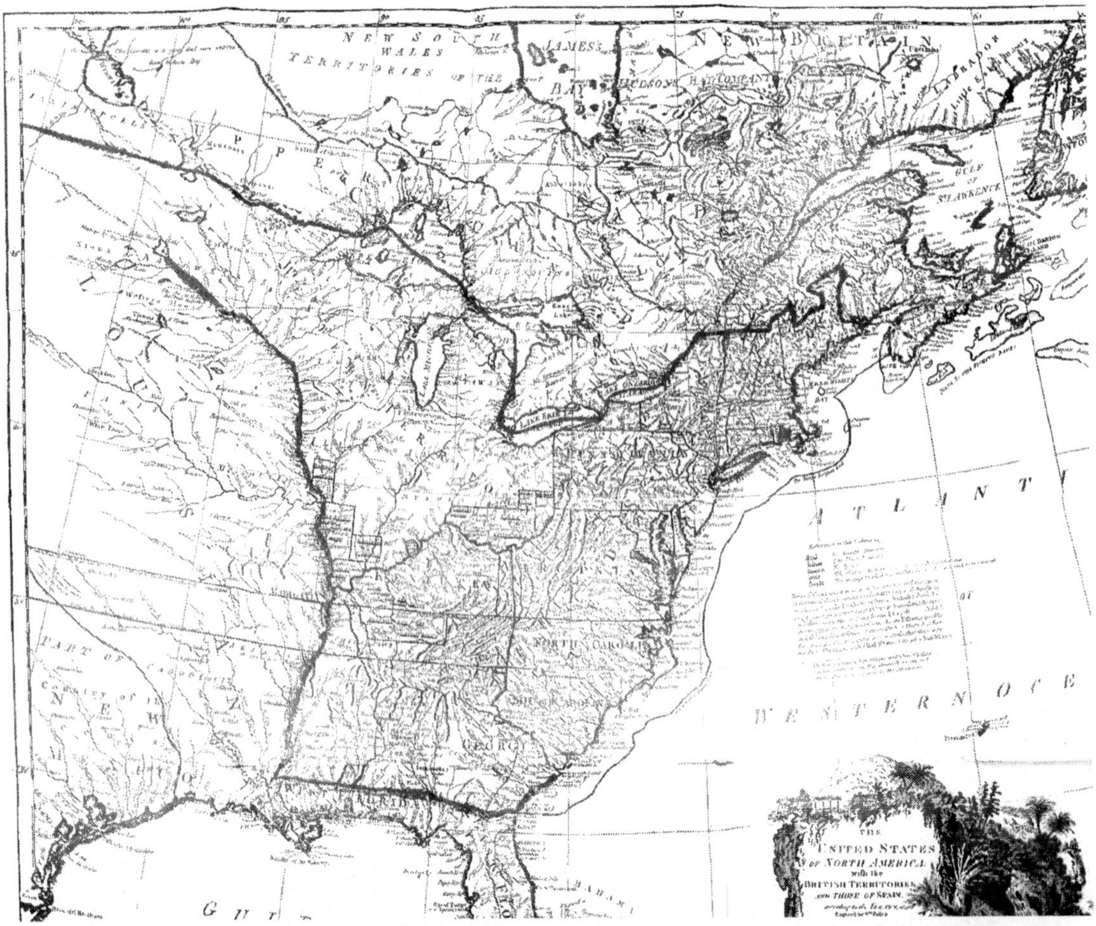
NEW SOUTH WALES
TERRITORIES OF THE
HUDSON'S BAY COMPANY
LABRADOR
GULF OF ST. LAWRENCE
LAKE ERIE
ATLANTIC
WESTERN OCEAN
NORTH CAROLINA
PART OF
THE
UNITED STATES
OF NORTH AMERICA
with the
BRITISH TERRITORIES
AND THOSE OF SPAIN.